VETSCHOOL

W9-BNS-856

The *Art* of Reading ▪

READING IS

THE ART

FUNDAMENTAL®

OF READING

Forty Illustrators Celebrate RIF's 40*th* *Anniversary*

WITH A FOREWORD BY LEONARD S. MARCUS

DUTTON BOOKS

DUTTON BOOKS

A member of Penguin Group (USA) Inc.

Published by the Penguin Group

Penguin Group (USA) Inc., 375 Hudson Street, New York, New York 10014, U.S.A. / Penguin Group (Canada), 10 Alcorn Avenue, Toronto, Ontario, Canada M4V 3B2 (a division of Pearson Penguin Canada Inc.) / Penguin Books Ltd, 80 Strand, London WC2R 0RL, England / Penguin Ireland, 25 St Stephen's Green, Dublin 2, Ireland (a division of Penguin Books Ltd) / Penguin Group (Australia), 250 Camberwell Road, Camberwell, Victoria 3124, Australia (a division of Pearson Australia Group Pty Ltd) / Penguin Books India Pvt Ltd, 11 Community Centre, Panchsheel Park, New Delhi - 110 017, India / Penguin Group (NZ), Cnr Airborne and Rosedale Roads, Albany, Auckland 1310, New Zealand (a division of Pearson New Zealand Ltd) / Penguin Books (South Africa) (Pty) Ltd, 24 Sturdee Avenue, Rosebank, Johannesburg 2196, South Africa / Penguin Books Ltd, Registered Offices: 80 Strand, London WC2R 0RL, England

This collection copyright © 2005 by Reading Is Fundamental®
The text and artwork in this book are the copyrighted property of their respective authors and illustrators. All rights reserved.

CIP Data is available.

Published in the United States by Dutton Books,
a member of Penguin Group (USA) Inc.
345 Hudson Street, New York, New York 10014
www.penguin.com/youngreaders

DESIGNED BY HEATHER WOOD
Manufactured in China / First Edition / ISBN 0-525-47484-6
10 9 8 7 6 5 4 3 2

Jacket art copyright © by Fred Marcellino. Used with permission of Pippin Properties, Inc. for the Estate of Fred Marcellino.
Image from the 1992 Children's Book Week poster © The Children's Book Council, Inc.,
a part of the collection of The Central Children's Room, Donnell Library Center, The New York Public Library

Title-page art copyright © 2005 by Patricia Polacco

page 11: Illustration copyright © 2005 by Tony DiTerlizzi

page 39: Patricia Polacco photo © Kenn Klein

page 52: Peter Sís photo © Palma Fiacco Fotografin

page 60: William Joyce's artwork for this book is based on Where the Wild Things Are, *by Maurice Sendak,*
copyright © 1963 by Maurice Sendak, copyright renewed 1991 by Maurice Sendak

page 63: Paul O. Zelinsky's artwork for this book is based on The Color Kittens, *by Margaret Wise Brown,*
copyright © 1958, copyright renewed 1986 by Random House, Inc. Used by permission of Golden Books,
an imprint of Random House Children's Books, a division of Random House, Inc.

The Publisher would like to thank the bookstores specializing in out-of-print, rare, and used books
that assisted in locating some of the titles mentioned here, with special thanks to Margaret Cooper of Browse About Books
in North Wilkesboro, North Carolina (nccoopers@earthlink.net) and Bill Montague and Jenny Goetz
of Fahrenheit's Books of Denver, Colorado (www.fahrenheitsbooks.com).

Special thanks also to Anne J. Hofmann, Chief Librarian of the Donnell Library Center, New York Public Library.

Special thanks are due to Aaron Smith and Kevin Fry for creating the Art of Reading project, to Leonard Marcus for his expert guidance and advice,
and to the staff and Board of Directors at the Corcoran Gallery of Art for hosting the event. The project would not have been a success without the assistance of hundreds
of dedicated RIF staff and volunteers. Thanks also to the RIF Board of Directors, especially Loretta Barrett and Lynda Johnson Robb, for lending their time,
devotion, and expertise to this effort. RIF is grateful to Dutton Children's Books for their willingness to publish this book,
support RIF's 40th anniversary, and extend the joy of reading to children and families across America.

To the artists

whose imagination and hard work

introduce millions of children

to the joys of books

■

Reading Is Fundamental is proud to join Dutton Books to present to America's children and families this special—and spectacular—book, created on the occasion of RIF's fortieth anniversary.

For four decades, RIF has touched tens of millions of young lives, providing well over 250 million free books to children in every corner of the country. By ensuring that America's children have access to books and to the astonishing worlds and wondrous ideas contained within them, RIF has sought to create a nation of eager, lifelong readers and productive citizens. By purchasing this book and sharing it with the children in your life, you are participating in RIF's quest to open the minds of young people to the transforming power of the reading experience.

This, of course, is a book about books. It's also a book about the ability of children's literature to change lives and open hearts. Each of the forty illustrators represented here was asked to re-imagine a favorite book from their own childhood that propelled them along their life's path of reading, writing, and creating. Illustrators, perhaps more than most of us, truly understand the power of art and imagination to inspire young readers to develop reading skills and begin a love affair with books that will last a lifetime. The forty works of art contained in these pages are a testament not only to the artists' skill but to the extraordinary ability of illustration to serve as a gateway to the world of books.

In a sense, this is a collection of memories, drawn from the childhood experiences of forty very special, very creative people. We hope it also serves as a springboard for fresh memories for a new generation of children—and the adults who help shape their lives.

The process of creating this book began in September 2003 at the RIF National Reading Celebration, when twenty-three of the illustrators featured in these pages interacted face-to-face with twenty thousand children and their families at the Corcoran Gallery of Art in Washington, D.C. Seventeen more have since joined us to complete this commemorative volume and to help celebrate RIF's fortieth birthday.

On behalf of the entire RIF family, profound thanks are offered to these remarkably talented illustrators. Their generosity of time, talent, and spirit, and their devotion to the future of America's children, are deeply appreciated.

RIF is also grateful to you for selecting this book and contributing to RIF's efforts to bring books and literacy services to millions of children and families in underserved areas of the country. We hope you will enjoy this celebration of art and reading and that it will lead you and the young people you share it with into new worlds, fresh discoveries, and cherished memories.

Carol H. Rasco

Carol H. Rasco
PRESIDENT AND CEO
READING IS FUNDAMENTAL®

Contents

The forty artists you are about to meet were once forty children learning to read, write, hold a paintbrush, and wonder about things.

Foreword

They came to the "art of reading"—illustration—from a diversity of places and backgrounds and beginnings: New York, Vermont, the Midwest, South Korea, the Netherlands; from homes well supplied with children's books and from homes and communities where reading matter of any kind was rare. Some were lucky enough to be read to by parents or teachers or befriended by librarians who took their interests to heart. Others met books on their own and in their own good time. Some simply took to reading while others had to struggle. One artist from the latter group, Patricia Polacco, recalls the deep personal connection she felt upon encountering the hero of Dr. Seuss's *Horton Hatches the Egg,* whose amusing example of fierce determination was enough to charm her into not giving up on books—at least not on books with pictures.

It is a fact worth noting that children with such wildly differing first experiences with the printed word all found their way to a love of books. And it is fascinating to learn how often one particular book made all the difference, and to realize that all sorts of books can have that life-changing potential.

Fortunately, many of the childhood favorites revisited in the pages that follow can still be found at the library or in bookstores. If *The Art of Reading* inspires you or a child you know to search out some of them, so much the better! Some are "classics" you may already know intimately: *Black Beauty, Where the Wild Things Are, The Cricket in Times Square,* and (the choice of two artists) *Charlotte's Web.* Why, *The Art of Reading* invites everyone to ask, do books such as these somehow last and last? Recalling his enthrallment with Walter R. Brooks's *Freddy the Detective,* Kevin Hawkes gives us his answer: "[*Freddy*] was my first experience with fantasy fiction," yet the story's hero—a talking pig, a sleuth with a curly pink tail—"seemed more real to me than any other character I had ever met. I began wondering what else in the world was more than it appeared to be."

Who could ask for better? Yet one child's *Freddy* will be some other child's long, sullen yawn, and that is as it should be, too. The classics don't need our veneration.

They need only to be loved by readers in whom they happen to strike a bright and responsive chord. Caldecott medalist Richard Egielski loved comic books, "any kind of comic book." He tells us here what happened when, as a young teen, he devoured the Classic Comics edition of *Moby Dick*. The excitement of it all merely whetted his appetite. In an effort to satisfy that hunger, he watched the movie version of Melville's epic on television. And then he read Melville.

Sometimes, young people do know best. As the author and artist Robert Lawson once observed: "No one can possibly tell what tiny detail of a drawing or what seemingly trivial phrase in a story will be the spark that sets off a great flash in the mind of some child, a flash that will leave a glow there until the day he dies."

Here, then, are forty sparks to read by.

—*Leonard S. Marcus*

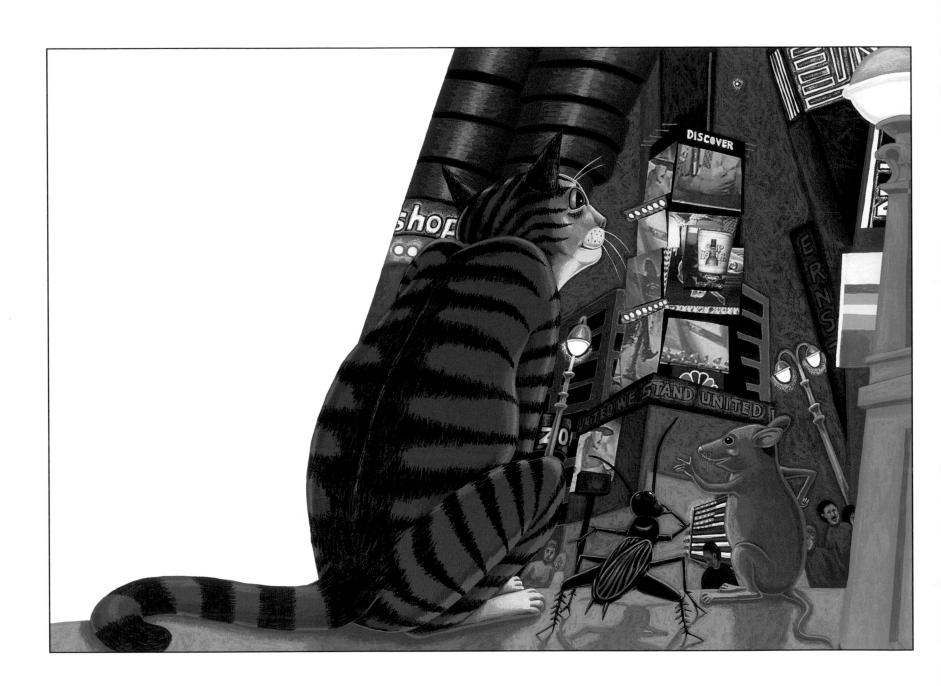

Nina Laden

Books were big to me when I was a kid. Art was big. New York City was really big. I lived in Queens with my artist parents. We rode the subway into Manhattan all the time. We went to a lot of museums, galleries, and the giant public library on Fifth Avenue. Everything in the city was huge to me, and full of mystery. I felt a lot like Chester, the cricket in George Selden's *The Cricket in Times Square*.

Chester finds himself in the Times Square subway station, after falling out of a picnic basket. He's from the country in Connecticut. He's small, and he's lost. But Chester makes friends with a mouse named Tucker, a cat named Harry, and a little boy named Mario . . . and the world doesn't seem so scary after all.

I loved this book as a child, and I still do as an adult. It shows that you can find magic and kindness in this world, even in the most unlikely places. I think the original Garth Williams pen-and-ink drawings are wonderful . . . but I wanted to bring Times Square, as Chester first sees it, alive in its colorful, collage glory. I altered the perspective so the reader could be right there with Harry, Chester, and Tucker as they come out of the station.

Writing and illustrating children's books was a dream of mine from an early age. I feel blessed to be able to tell my stories, bring them to life, and create a complete world between two covers. I was inspired by books like *The Cricket in Times Square*. Books feed my imagination, and my imagination fuels my books. Feed yours a steady diet.

Nina Laden lived in Queens when she was young and rode the subway into Manhattan with her parents all the time.

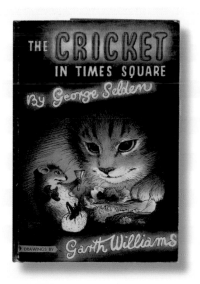

Newbery Honor Book **The Cricket in Times Square,** *by George Selden and illustrated by Garth Williams, was published in 1960.*

Ashley Bryan has been inspired his whole life by the spirituals, songs of musical genius created by black slaves.

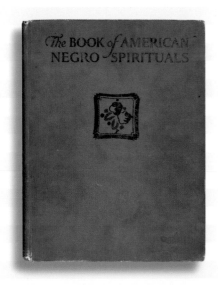

This copy of **The Book of American Negro Spirituals** *was published in 1925. A gift to Ashley Bryan from a friend, it is a treasured family heirloom.*

Ashley Bryan

The African-American spirituals are loved and sung throughout the world. They are considered America's finest gift to world music. I have loved hearing, learning, and singing these songs from childhood to the present day.

An important collection of the spirituals by James Weldon Johnson and J. Rosamond Johnson, *The Book of American Negro Spirituals*, was published by The Viking Press in 1925. It is, however, from hearing the spirituals sung that I have been inspired to create so many of the images in my artwork.

In the United States, people sing spirituals. They generally do not know that these songs were created by black slaves because they are not taught historically. Wherever I travel in the United States I ask the children in the school assemblies, "Does anyone know a spiritual?" I give the songs all the names for which they are known—Negro spirituals, African-American spirituals, Black American spirituals. No hands go up. However, when I start singing "He's Got the Whole World in His Hands," they sing me down. The same for "This Little Light of Mine" and "When the Saints Go Marching In." I say these songs are spirituals and were created by black slaves.

Under the oppressive force of slavery that denied blacks the right to learn to read or write, the enslaved blacks found a way to be creative. They created thousands of songs called spirituals. The names of the individual composers of the words and the melodies have been lost, but we know that these songs come from the musical genius of black slaves.

In the sixties, when I studied in France and Germany, the students sang spirituals, and they knew the historical background of the songs. They gave me books of their folk songs that were published regularly. They asked me to send them introductory books of the spirituals when I returned home. After my return, I was surprised to find that there were no introductory books of these songs.

Over the years I have worked on five books of spirituals that have been published. My hope is that children growing up with introductory books of the spirituals will create books, as adults, so that the spirituals will make their appearance regularly, just as new presentations of Mother Goose, ABC, and counting books are published regularly. I have chosen "Mary Had a Baby" and "Ride On, King Jesus" to illustrate for the Reading Is Fundamental project. The spirit of these songs is at the heart of everything I do. I stand up through this ancestral gift, the freedom of creative expression.

Ashley Wolff remembers picking wild blueberries with her mother as a child growing up in Vermont.

Blueberries for Sal, *by Robert McCloskey, a Caldecott Honor Book, was first published in 1948.*

Ashley Wolff

We love some books because they let us experience the foreign and exotic. They take us away from our normal lives. I loved this book because it felt so *close* to my own life. As a child, I felt as if I *was* Sal.

Like her, I grew up in New England. Not in Maine, where *Blueberries for Sal* takes place, but—close by—in Vermont. I, too, picked wild blueberries with my mother on "Blueberry Hill." Dressed in droopy overalls, with a shaggy, homemade haircut and barefoot sandals with cutouts over the toes, we even looked alike. Even Sal's family car was just like our car: Moby Dick, a big, white boat of a station wagon.

When I read *Blueberries for Sal* as a child, it felt totally real. Although I had never seen anything more dangerous than a woodchuck when out berry picking, it seemed perfectly reasonable to me that a four-year-old girl could follow an eight-hundred-pound black bear, thinking it was her mother.

First published in 1948 and continuously in print ever since, *Blueberries for Sal* was one of eight books that Robert McCloskey wrote and illustrated in the 1940s and '50s. I know that many were autobiographical because I was lucky enough to meet both Mr. McCloskey and his grown daughter Sal at a conference.

I've long thought that this is a perfect picture book in the sense that the rhythm, pacing, and impeccable conclusion form a package that is both elegant and completely satisfying. The artwork, in brush and dark blue ink, is so robust and well drawn that no one notices there is no color.

I chose to re-imagine a part of the book that is often rushed past in the hurry to get to the story: the endpaper. The only interior scene in the book, the endpaper shows an old-fashioned kitchen, with wood-burning stove and Sal's serene mother calmly pouring hot blueberries into a canning jar while Sal strings rubber canning rings onto a wooden spoon.

The very notion of canning was quite foreign to my modern 1960s mom and me. We never picked enough berries to can, and if we had—we would have frozen ours.

For my piece, in *The Art of Reading,* I wondered what that scene would look like in a city kitchen with all the modern conveniences of today.

18 ■ *The Art of Reading*

Lois Ehlert traces her love of color, shape, and creating with her hands to her mother, who was a good seamstress, and her father, who had a basement workshop.

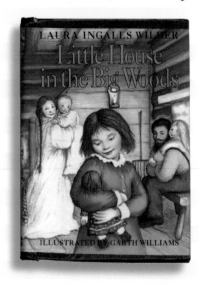

Little House in the Big Woods, *by Laura Ingalls Wilder, illustrated by Garth Williams, was first published in 1932.*

Lois Ehlert

I grew up in a small town. No bookstore. No art museum. But my mother, my younger brother and sister, and I went to the library once a week, picked out books, read them all, and returned for more. My favorite book was a chapter book that Mom read to us, called *Little House in the Big Woods,* by Laura Ingalls Wilder, a story situated in early Wisconsin, my home state. What I remember best were the loving descriptions of the land and a sense of place. That's what I strive for when I write and illustrate books today, so many years later—a sense of place and respect for the earth.

This illustration is based on art created for *Waiting for Wings,* a book I wrote and illustrated about flowers and butterflies. I began by painting watercolor washes on sheets of bond paper, creating texture by crinkling some of the paper while the watercolor was still wet. When the paint was dry, I added double-sided adhesive to the back of each sheet. Then I began cutting shapes out of the colored papers, gluing them together on a board, like pieces of a puzzle, to form a picture. This technique is called collage.

Lynne Cherry

How the Mole Got His Pockets, by Eduard Petiška, with illustrations by Zdeněk Miler, was my favorite book when I was a child. A mole burrows through the ground, collects many treasures, and wishes he had some pockets to put them in!

I lost my copy, but I have vivid memories of this book's bright colors and an adorable, imaginative, creative mole's plan to make overalls. One animal friend cuts the flax, another beats and softens it, another peels its threads, and another weaves the threads into cloth. The crayfish cuts the cloth, and a weaverbird sews it.

As a child I was fascinated by the process—how each small step gets us closer to accomplishing a task, learning a skill, or making something—whether it's learning to ride a bicycle, painting a picture, or making overalls with the help of friends!

This book showed me the connection between my life and the natural world; I learned that some plants provide fiber for making and others for dyeing cloth, so I became more curious about and observant of individual plants—and I began to draw them.

Reading *How the Mole Got His Pockets* again and again as a child inspired me to write and illustrate stories and create characters of my own. Certainly Little Groundhog in *How Groundhog's Garden Grew* would have found a friend in the industrious mole. *The Shaman's Apprentice* is about how plants are used by rain-forest peoples. Every plant in *The Great Kapok Tree* is a recognizable plant. And a garden is also the setting for *Where Butterflies Grow*.

Why did twenty thousand people come to the RIF/Corcoran event to watch children's illustrators? Watching a piece of art appear from a blank piece of paper right before one's eyes is rather magical and mysterious. I am often as surprised to see the end result as a stranger would be watching me paint. It is fascinating to watch all the small steps—tiny lines and brushstrokes—that go into the creation of an illustration.

Those who watch us realized that it does take a lot of time and patience to create illustrations, but that the process is fun and the end result rewarding (or amazing!). But it takes practice to get good at anything. So, kids, parents . . . I hope you'll turn off that TV, go outside, sit quietly in a natural place, take in the beauty of nature, and try your hand at drawing, too!

Reading How the Mole Got His Pockets *again and again as a child inspired Lynne Cherry to write and illustrate stories and create characters of her own.*

How the Mole Got His Pockets, *written by Eduard Petiška and illustrated by Zdeněk Miler, was first published in Czechoslovakia in 1974 and is now out of print. This copy was found at Fahrenheit's Books of Denver, Colorado.*

Raúl Colón was born in New York City and as a child loved to imagine the faces of characters he'd read about in books.

The Legend of Sleepy Hollow, *by Washington Irving, was published in 1820. This facsimile edition of the original, with illustrations by Arthur Rackham, was published in 1990.*

Raúl Colón

When I was in third grade, I met a headless horseman. He appeared before me in a book I was reading, *The Legend of Sleepy Hollow*. Written by Washington Irving in the early nineteenth century, this book fueled my imagination and scared me out of my wits.

I guess kids today wouldn't be as frightened as I was, what with all the horror movies and video games they're familiar with these days. But the great thing about a story like *The Legend of Sleepy Hollow* is that you can make up your own scary scenes as you read along. For instance, I made up the characters' faces as I read their descriptions. If there was a line or two about a pretty girl with rosy, red cheeks and a beautiful smile, I could put that face together in my own mind. If a character was described as tall and skinny with a long nose, I could construct those features using my imagination as well. All the smells, all the colors, all the emotions that were put into words looked and felt so real when I re-imagined them. Well, that's what reading does for you. If writers do their job well, they'll place a bunch of pictures in your head. It's almost as if you were making your own movie, except there's no camera—only you and your brain and the page.

Artists live for the chance to dwell deep inside their minds and create images that no one's seen before. It's like sailing into some other universe, away from the one we experience every day, to find something extraordinarily new: another world.

Even though, as an illustrator, I perfected my skills with constant practice, reading played a part as I learned my craft. Drawing skills alone are not enough. Great ideas are what put the best artists over the top. Reading helps develop those ideas. That's why I always remember that headless horseman who, years ago, scared the living daylights out of me and triggered my imagination and opened other doors in my head. Out of those doors pours the stream of images I draw today. Hey, I even get paid to draw them. So I say, thank you, Mr. Horseman, you've been a great help.

Steven Kellogg

When I was beginning the third grade, an aunt gave me a birthday membership in a book club, which made it possible for me to receive a new book in the mail every month for one year. The first one to arrive was *Black Beauty*, by Anna Sewell, and I was wild about it. First published in 1877, the book brought to life the pre-automotive days when everyone kept horses, and I, as a fanatical animal lover, wanted to live in that world!

The story is told by the main character, a horse named Black Beauty, and through his observations of the life around him, the author expresses her feelings about the range of treatment to which horses were subjected. She warmly describes owners who are considerate and kind while exposing and deploring the insensitivity and cruelty of others. The book had a major impact when it was published, and it brought about a wave of support for the humane treatment of animals.

My favorite horse was a chestnut mare named Ginger, who meets Black Beauty early in the book when the two find themselves under new ownership and sharing a serene pasture. Ginger is a beautiful, high-spirited horse, but she tells a story of a harsh early life during which she rebelled against the cruel handling by her owners. She hopes that she and Black Beauty can remain together in their current, congenial environment where the new owner is trying to rehabilitate her and to gently gain her trust. However, before long, circumstances cause the horses to be sold separately.

Much later Ginger and Black Beauty briefly meet again in a chapter entitled "Poor Ginger." Time and hard use have taken their toll on both of them, and they have been reduced to a life of drudgery, hauling cabs in congested London traffic. Ginger, however, has been so changed by her suffering that Black Beauty hardly recognizes her, and he is saddened to realize that the spirit of his once proud and beautiful friend has been broken by a succession of cruel and abusive owners.

Shortly afterward he catches a last glimpse of her lying dead on the back of a passing cart.

As a young reader, I admired Ginger's independence and her determination to rebel against unfair treatment. The drawing of her sad, broken figure at the head of the last chapter in my edition of *Black Beauty* moved me very deeply, and I have chosen to re-imagine it for this book. I remember wishing that I could have returned Ginger to the beautiful pasture where she briefly found friendship and hope. So I have painted myself as a third grader accomplishing that wish to liberate Ginger, and I have restored her to the spirited, young horse that she had been when I first met her early in the story.

As a young reader, Steven Kellogg admired Ginger's independence and her determination to rebel against unfair treatment.

Written by Anna Sewell and first published in 1877, **Black Beauty** *brought to life the pre-automotive days when everyone kept horses. Steven Kellogg, as a fanatical animal lover, wanted to live in that world.*

David McPhail owned hundreds of comic books as a child. They cost a dime apiece, and he could get ten cents at the corner store in exchange for two soda-pop bottles.

The Five Chinese Brothers, *by Claire Huchet Bishop, illustrated by Kurt Wiese, is a dramatic retelling of an old Chinese tale. It was published in 1938.*

David McPhail

I grew up near the ocean, and on most sunny summer days my mother would take us—my sister, my brothers, and me—to the beach. I didn't understand the tides at all, and I was fascinated by them. At high tide, most of the beach was submerged. But at low tide, the ocean retreated, leaving shallow tide pools and shell-strewn sandbars for us to explore.

Sometimes I imagined what it would be like if the ocean just kept going, if it receded beyond the horizon and left the entire seafloor exposed, with sunken ships and pirate treasure lying all about. How exciting that would be! I would wander the ocean bottom, filling my pail with gold coins and exotic shells.

Around that time, on a visit to the local library, I discovered *The Five Chinese Brothers,* by Claire Huchet Bishop. That was the first time in my young life that I felt the author was speaking directly to, and even about, me. The story both excited and alarmed me, and I was especially fascinated with the Brother who could swallow the sea. That was the beginning of my relationship with books.

Still, books were not a big part of my life. When I was young, there was too much else to do. There were friends and siblings to play with; there was drawing, my train set, baseball, my bow and arrow, and my drums. In the evenings I listened to my favorite radio programs, and on Saturday afternoons I went to the movies. When I did read, I read comic books. I had hundreds of them stacked on my bureau and under my bed.

During my junior year of high school, my interest in books was rekindled by my English teacher, Mr. Ryan, who loved literature. When he read aloud from *Two Years Before the Mast,* by Richard Henry Dana, I felt a connection that I hadn't felt since I'd first picked up *The Five Chinese Brothers.* I began to look for other books in which I could lose myself and discovered John Steinbeck, Sinclair Lewis, and Kenneth Roberts. I read everything I could find by these authors.

Lately it has struck me that I can't possibly live long enough to read all the books I want to read. In a way, it's a comfort to know that I'll never run out of reading material.

3rd Day

Ahab

Richard Egielski

My road to many of the great classic novels often started by first seeing the movie version on television. I saw the movie of *The Wizard of Oz* long before I read the book. The same with *A Christmas Carol, The Hunchback of Notre Dame, Dracula, Frankenstein*, and others. But *Moby Dick* was a little bit different. When I was a kid, I loved comic books—any kind of comic book. One day I was in my local soda shop/comic shop, and on the rack I see this one comic with a big, white whale on the cover. The series was called Classic Comics, and this one was *Moby Dick*. I plunked down my twelve cents and bought it. Okay, the comic lacked the complexities and symbolism of Herman Melville's novel, but it still came across as a very cool adventure story. I loved the characters Queequeg and Ishmael and Ahab. Then I saw the movie, which again lacked the complexities and symbolism of the book, but it still was an exciting story. *Then* I read the book and, being a young teenager, I didn't get all the complexities and symbolism of the novel, but I drew pictures of the ship, the characters, and the whale. Drawing pictures from books was my way of living in the story and lengthening my time with books I loved. That's probably how I came to be a book illustrator. A few years ago I reread *Moby Dick*. I still didn't get all the complexities and symbolism, but I still love the great fish tale.

Richard Egielski loved comic books as a kid and first met Moby Dick *in the pages of Classic Comics.*

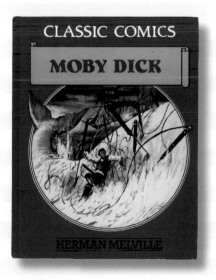

This hardcover edition of Classic Comics: Moby Dick *was published in 1991.*

The day she started her illustration for this book, Diana Cain Bluthenthal found this web-writing spider at work in her garden.

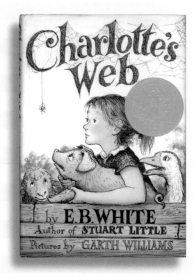

Garth Williams illustrated Charlotte's Web, *by E. B. White, and many other classic books in his long and illustrious career.*

Diana Cain Bluthenthal

I didn't have any pets growing up. My parents didn't want the fuss. I had two plants and a brief encounter once with sea monkeys.

I started to carry pussy willows in my pockets. They were my pets. When their fur fell off, I was so upset. I was truly a child in need of something to love and something to love me.

Fern, in E. B. White's *Charlotte's Web*, begins the book by asking her mother at breakfast one morning, "Where's Papa going with that ax?"

"Out to the hoghouse," her mother replies. "Some pigs were born last night."

Fern dashes out the door, across the dewy wet grass, to the barnyard to stop her father from taking the life of the smallest "runt" pig.

I ran in my mind, too, just like Fern. And I continued to read, and react, as if I were one of E. B. White's characters. I was as horrified as Wilbur to think of Charlotte as bloodthirsty. And I was as amazed as Wilbur to learn from Charlotte's no-nonsense personality, her courage, her intelligence, and her loyalty as a friend.

Garth Williams's drawings were magical to me. I'm sure they were an early influence on my wanting to become a children's illustrator. Mr. Williams breathed a life into the farm and its characters beyond words. His portrayal on page six of Fern bottle-feeding Wilbur in her lap was my favorite picture.

Of course, now grown with my own family, we can and do have pets. I've never been accused of having a farm, but once my husband did say to me the place was becoming a zoo.

Now joining our family of four are two dogs, Puck and Peaches, a small, green snake named Ribbons, two very sweet pet rats, Clover and Blossom, and a large tank of fish.

Other "pets" in our home on the summer catch-and-release program have included toads, frogs, salamanders, caterpillars, a skink (that's a lizard), a turtle, crickets, ants (in a farm), and worms (yes, worms). I'm proud to say that no critter has perished under my watch, and I've become quite good at catching flies. Also, as a military family, we've lived near all kinds of animals across the United States, from foxes and deer to pelicans and barracuda. I feel very lucky.

Upon this writing, there is a large black-and-yellow spider we've named *Charlotte* who's spun her web on the back of our shed. She's really some spider. Just terrific. You could even say *radiant*.

Henry Cole

I was lucky to have the best third-grade teacher ever, Dot Patterson, who read installments of *Charlotte's Web* to my class after lunch. Also, I grew up on a farm outside a small town, much like the setting of Fern Avery's farm in *Charlotte's Web*. E. B. White's story of Fern, and of the animals on the farm, filled me with emotion. I recall putting my head down on my desk to stifle my agony at the end of chapter twenty-one! And though I was not an avid reader, I remember feeling the power of the story, even at that early age, as *Charlotte's Web* was read aloud to us. I felt that Charlotte had the wisdom and patience of my mother; Fern reminded me of my sister Trish; and the personalities of Wilbur, Templeton, and the other characters in the book were as familiar and comforting as real live people.

I also loved Garth Williams's drawings; they're filled with sensitivity, warmth, humor, and intelligence. For this project, I decided to make a cover for the book, although Mr. Williams's original cover could never be improved.

Incidentally, Miss Patterson was the first to ask me to illustrate a story. She told us shortly before Christmas that year to create a picture for *The Littlest Angel,* and I still remember the excitement and satisfaction of that assignment.

Henry Cole was first asked to illustrate a story by his third-grade teacher, Dot Patterson.

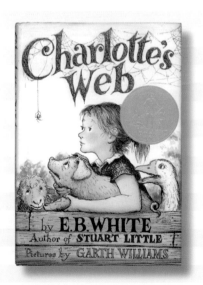

Charlotte's Web, *by E. B. White, illustrated by Garth Williams, was a Newbery Honor Book in 1953.*

Eric Rohmann

I first read *Millions of Cats* when I was eight years old and thought I'd never seen a book so strange and so beautiful. I still marvel at the expressive black-and-white line drawings, the inventive compositions, and the millions and billions and trillions of cats. The story is both hilarious and unexpected. Reading *Millions of Cats* for the first time made me realize that there are people out there like me. I thought, maybe I can make a picture book, too.

Near the end of *Millions of Cats*, we see a drawing of the very old man and the very old woman, their backs to the reader, looking out of the window of a cozy, little house. Outside, the millions and billions and trillions of cats, who had sipped all the water out of the pond and eaten every blade of grass on the hills, now scratched and clawed and made a great noise.

> But after a while the noise stopped and the very old man and the very old woman peeped out the window to see what had happened. They could not see a single cat! "I think they must have eaten each other all up," said the very old woman. "It's too bad!"

Wanda Gág makes a deal with her readers: I'll tell you a story if you agree to play along. She trusted me to seize what was on the page and make it real by participating in the story. Her trust allowed me to make the leap of absurdity—millions and billions and trillions of cats scratching and clawing and, in the end, eating "each other all up." But Gág chose not to illustrate that moment. Was it too gruesome, too shocking, too unbelievable? Perhaps, but I think illustrating the moment would have simply given too much information. By leaving it out, Gág showed me a doorway into the story, carrying me beyond my expectations. *Millions of Cats* gave me just enough information to light the fire of my own imaginings. When I was eight, I recall making a little drawing of the moment just after the quarreling, scratching, and clawing: a drawing of the only cat left standing, enormous and satisfied!

Painter, printmaker, and fine-book maker Eric Rohmann creates hand-colored relief prints on his printing press.

Newbery Honor Book Millions of Cats, *by Wanda Gág, published in 1928, gave Eric Rohmann just enough information to light the fire of his own imaginings.*

Jerry Pinkney can vividly recall listening to his parents and their friends as they sat in the backyard trading stories on warm summer nights.

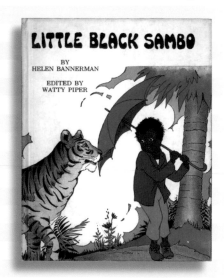

Little Black Sambo, by Helen Bannerman, was first published in 1899.

Jerry Pinkney

I grew up in a small row house in Philadelphia, Pennsylvania, the fourth child, having two older brothers, an older sister, and two younger sisters. One could say I was the middle child. Our modest home library consisted of a varied mix of titles. However, the art of oral storytelling was very much a part of our day-to-day social fabric. I can vividly recall the richest of those times and how these narratives would entertain and inform us children.

I shared a bedroom with my brothers. Our room was located in the rear of a second-floor landing that overlooked our backyard. At one time the wooden slatted fences separating the yards were removed. This created a communal setting, perfect for telling stories. I would lie in bed on warm nights with raised windows, listening to Mother, Dad, and their friends enjoy the act of trading tales. Their accountings spoke of the ups and downs of daily life, journey stories of their migration from southern farms, family stories, and, for me, most significantly, folklore. There were animated stories like "The Tales of Uncle Remus" and "The Legend of John Henry." Oftentimes I would conjure up pictures in my mind to accompany those all-important tales that were rooted in their experiences of living in the South.

I was inspired to exercise my imagination further and create other pictures. As a result, I drew throughout those growing years. Were the seeds sowed at that time responsible for my growth into a visual storyteller? One can only wonder.

Within the small collection of books in our home, there was a Bible and an edition of Ralph Waldo Emerson, which my mother was often found reading. Also, she would read classic fairy tales by Hans Christian Andersen and stories like *Aesop's Fables* to the younger members of our family.

However, of all the books in our home, there was only one with a child of color. It became my favorite—*Little Black Sambo*, by Helen Bannerman—a story about a boy of color who exhibited courage and wit. For me, he was a hero wearing clothing of the coolest of colors, who triumphed over menacing, foolish tigers. I revisited *Little Black Sambo* more than fifty years later, when I illustrated a retelling in collaboration with author Julius Lester. As a result of my dyslexia, the written word is always a challenge for me. Nevertheless, when I was a child, I understood, even then, the power and wonder of a tale well told. A good story may enlarge and inform our understanding of ourselves and others. Like the many colors of a brave young boy's school clothing, good stories brighten our lives.

Patricia Polacco

Horton Hatches the Egg, by Dr. Seuss, is a book that truly impacted my young life. The improbable animals with their mirthful, expressive faces enchanted me. And dear faithful, reliable, dependable Horton the elephant. He climbed onto that skinny, little limb that could hardly support his bulk without a second thought as to whether or not it could hold him. Then he carefully sat on something so fragile—a tiny bird's egg—never considering that he might break it! This helped me realize what faith in oneself is all about! The heart of the story is also about making a promise and keeping it . . . no matter what may come. He stayed on that little nest through the most horrific happenings. He never gave up!

Then he was rewarded by hatching out a creature transformed from what was ordinary into a new creation. Unusual, new to the world and the universe. I wanted to be just like Horton, and as it turns out, being an author-illustrator is all about transforming the ordinary into the unusual and creating new worlds and universes that never existed before. And, of course, never . . . ever . . . giving up on even the most improbable idea!

Even though I had great difficulty reading, I loved poring over the pictures in books. My favorite, of course, was *Horton Hatches the Egg*. I could just see him sitting on that skinny, little branch. Then I started thinking . . . if Horton can sit on that skinny, little branch, then any elephant can, and that means I can! I tried it and fell soundly to the ground, out of my grandfather's small cherry tree. Although I was a little sore, it did not dampen my enthusiasm or belief in Horton and all elephants, for that matter!

As a matter of fact, because of Horton, I had an imaginary elephant for a playmate of my very own. Her name was Sweet Pea, and she went everywhere with me. Our family had to keep an empty chair at the table just for her! She rode in the back of the car with me, and we played secret games together. She even went to the doctor with me. She did wondrous things to help me not be so scared of him. I remember, on one visit to the doctor, he took her temperature and gave her a shot first. My favorite time with her was just sitting on the sofa and looking at books together. Horton was her favorite, too!

As the years have passed, I don't see her as much anymore. I would imagine that she is charming some other youngster right at this very moment with her lumbering and gentle ways. I'll bet they are reading *Horton Hatches the Egg* together!

Patricia Polacco comes from a family of great storytellers. She believes that when you are raised on hearing, rather than seeing, stories, you get very good at telling stories yourself.

One of many classic and beloved picture books written and illustrated by Dr. Seuss, Horton Hatches the Egg *was first published in 1940.*

40 ■ *The Art of Reading*

In 1969, Mary Azarian started Farmhouse Press in Vermont and began producing woodcut prints. She uses a nineteenth-century Vandercook proof press.

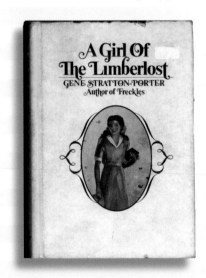

A Girl of the Limberlost, *by Gene Stratton-Porter, was first published in 1909 and has been available in many editions ever since.*

Mary Azarian

When I was eight years old, I read Gene Stratton-Porter's *A Girl of the Limberlost.* I was completely absorbed by the story, and I found it both comforting and inspiring. The main character is a sixteen-year-old girl, Elnora Comstock, who lets no obstacles come between her and her desire for an education. She is passionate about the wildlife that abounds in the Limberlost, a swamp near her modest cabin home. I grew up as an only child in the country and, like Elnora, I spent many hours exploring the woods and fields around our farm, so it was easy to identify with her.

I really hadn't thought about this book for many years and decided that I should reread it before I did an illustration. At first, the language and the characters seemed too old-fashioned, but the story soon took on a life of its own and brought back the same feelings I had when I read it as a child. This book is about following your passions and making the impossible happen. It was the first time I got "lost" in a book, and the experience sent me rushing to the library to find other books that would do the same for me. I credit *A Girl of the Limberlost* for helping me discover the magical world of books.

By the time he was in seventh grade, David Wiesner had seen all the great and not-so-great outer space and alien-invasion movies.

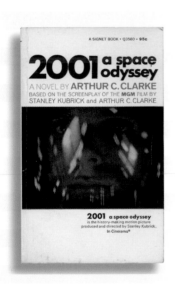

David Wiesner got his copy of 2001: A Space Odyssey, *by Arthur C. Clarke, through his school book club.*

It is impossible for me to talk about Arthur C. Clarke's novel *2001: A Space Odyssey* without talking about *2001: A Space Odyssey*, the movie, as well as the book *The Making of Kubrick's 2001*. My reactions to all three are forever intertwined.

David Wiesner

By the time I was in seventh grade, I had seen all the great and not-so-great outer space and alien-invasion movies—*Forbidden Planet, Invaders from Mars, The Angry Red Planet.* But none of those prepared me for the movie *2001: A Space Odyssey.* I was amazed, confused, and ultimately inspired by its visual impact.

Not too long after I saw the film, the novel *2001: A Space Odyssey* showed up in my school's book-club catalog. I decided that I had to read it. The book turned out to be as fantastic and absorbing as the movie, and I couldn't put it down. When I finished, I read it again. And as I did, I ran the movie through my head, fascinated by the way the same idea had been presented in two different mediums, one visual and one literary. The filmmaker offered no explanations and left the viewer to interpret the images; the writer guided the reader through the story and revealed the unspoken thoughts of the characters. For the first time, I began to think about not just the art but also the art form.

I got my chance to learn more about the collaboration of writer and filmmaker with my next book-club order. *The Making of Kubrick's 2001*, edited by Jerome Agel, turned out to be a nonfiction chronicle of the creative process of Arthur C. Clarke and director Stanley Kubrick. I was completely captivated by this book. For a kid who wanted to be an artist—though I couldn't have articulated that desire at the time—coming across a whole book devoted to artists working on their art was unbelievable. What's more, this wasn't about the ceiling of the Sistine Chapel and how Michelangelo painted it long ago; this was about an outer-space movie I had just seen and a science-fiction book I had just read. The story of how these two artists created their respective *2001*'s was, to me, as exciting as any adventure story.

Brian Selznick

This picture is a collaboration between me now, at age thirty-eight, and me at age fourteen. When I was fourteen, I did a report on *The Martian Chronicles*, which was my favorite book at the time (and remains one of my favorites). The book is a collection of short stories that form a narrative of man's first visits to Mars and the eventual colonization of the planet. I drew Ylla, the

Martian heroine in the opening story, who dreams of strange men from the uninhabitable planet Earth (too much oxygen to support life!) coming to visit Mars. She had golden eyes and, as you can see {at left}, I drew her in profile, with an exotic Martian headdress. I had also drawn her husband, Yll, with his scary mask and the weapon he uses to go kill the humans. For the current painting, I wanted to incorporate the characters I had envisioned when I was fourteen.

I still have my dog-eared copy of *The Martian Chronicles.* The artist who did the paintings on the front and the back chose an orange and red palette, and I realized after I began that I was using the same colors.

Also, when I was a kid I loved the work of Leonardo da Vinci, especially a painting called *The Madonna of the Rocks.* For Ylla's portrait in the current painting, I decided to pay homage to my childhood love of Leonardo. So besides using the drawing of Ylla that I did at fourteen as an inspiration, I also incorporated one of the faces from *The Madonna of the Rocks* {detail shown at left} into her portrait here. I loved the mysterious expression Leonardo captured so eloquently, and I wanted Ylla to have a little of that expression, too.

Brian Selznick found inspiration in the work of Leonardo da Vinci and still has a drawing he did of Leonardo's **The Madonna of the Rocks** *when he was ten.*

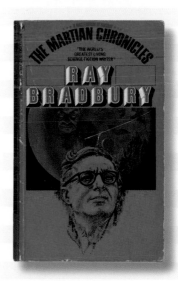

The science-fiction classic **The Martian Chronicles,** *by Ray Bradbury, was first published in 1950 and describes the colonization of Mars by humans.*

Paul Meisel loved to pore over the cartoons of Charles Addams as a child.

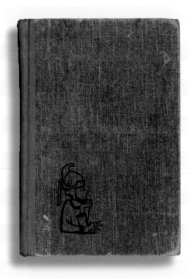

This copy of **The 13 Clocks**, *by James Thurber, illustrated by Marc Simont, originally belonged to Paul Meisel's brother, Ronald.*

Paul Meisel

The book that I chose to re-imagine is *The 13 Clocks*, by James Thurber, illustrated by Marc Simont. Published in 1950, this quirky tale of good and evil captured my imagination when I first read it at the age of eight. The Simont illustrations were different from anything that I had seen before. Accustomed to the cheerful worlds of Dr. Seuss, Garth Williams, Robert McCloskey, and others, I was taken by this dark and mysterious book, drawn with a simple elegance that I still find satisfying to look at.

The 13 Clocks depicts a dank castle world, complete with princes, a princess, spies, witches, and goofy (and sometimes invisible) sidekicks. The illustrations are funny in an offbeat way, similar to Thurber's writing style for this book. It was about the time that I came across *The 13 Clocks* that I happened upon a collection of *The New Yorker* cartoons and was immediately drawn to the world of Charles Addams. My parents also had a book of Saul Steinberg drawings, which I looked at repeatedly. Seeing the work of these great illustrators, cartoonists, and artists when I was young, along with many, many others over the years, certainly played a major role in this circuitous path that I have taken to where I am today.

P.S. This version of *The 13 Clocks* originally belonged to my brother. (I know this from the BIG block letters, RONALD, that he printed on the front endpapers.) After disappearing from his bookshelf many years ago, *The 13 Clocks* has been on my bookshelf from one move to another over these many years. (Only a boxed set of *The World of Pooh* and a copy of *The Hobbit* have that same distinction.) Someday, if he asks for it back, I'll return it! Maybe . . .

David Diaz

"When I stepped out into the bright sunlight from the darkness of the movie house . . ." is the first line and also the last line of S. E. Hinton's *The Outsiders*. Something about that symmetry, that circular motion of the story, has always appealed to me. Not an arch, but a circle in which, in the end, the characters emerge intact— altered by life and its knocks in numerous ways, but intact. *The Outsiders* fell into my hands through my older brother, who was reading it for his high school English class. I was in the sixth grade, living in Hollywood, Florida, when I read it for the first time. I remember that the cover of the book was red, and the letters in the title were done in an irregular, brushy font that I outlined with my pen, over and over, eventually obliterating most of the cover. I'm not sure if my brother told me that he liked it, or if I just decided on my own that I wanted to read it, one of several books that would be passed down to me. I lost myself in the story and came out thinking that there were books out there that spoke of a life I recognized. And that family is not only a bond of blood but a bond of love.

The characters had such wonderful names—Ponyboy, Sodapop, Two-Bit, and Dallas. I wanted a name like that, a name that defined who you were—not just the name itself, but also the sound of the name, the way it rolled off the tongue. I could relate to the struggle between the Socs—pronounced "soshes" and short for "socialites"—and the Greasers. It was not so far removed from the hardscrabble life and the life of privilege that existed in south Florida when I was growing up, and that I imagine still does today. Maybe that's why the story S. E. Hinton wrote when she was only sixteen years old turned out to be so timeless.

What I did then and still do, when I read today, is what most people do: picture the characters in my head. But when I illustrate, I'm more interested in trying to capture the essence of a character than the exact features described in the book. The challenge is to let those images stir around inside my head, and at the same time get myself out of the way so that I can bring them to life with my brush. The loose, brushy style I used in this drawing of Ponyboy and the rest of the outsiders is one I am very comfortable with. It allows me the freedom to interpret the characters in my own way.

When David Diaz was in the first grade, he knew he wanted to be an artist—although he had no idea what an illustrator, designer, or art director was.

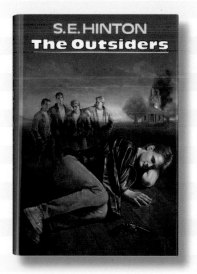

The Outsiders, *by S. E. Hinton, was published in 1967 and made into a movie of the same name, directed by Francis Coppola, in 1983.*

*Bryan Collier grew up in a house
that was filled with books.*

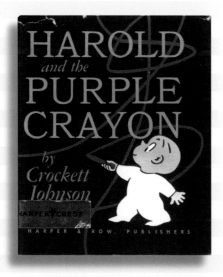

*Harold's wonderful purple crayon
makes everything he draws become real
in* Harold and the Purple Crayon, *by
Crockett Johnson, published in 1955.*

Bryan Collier

When I was a child, we had so many books at home. Our mother read to us all the time. One of my favorites was *Harold and the Purple Crayon*, by Crockett Johnson. I loved that story because, like Harold, I loved to draw. Harold drew his world just the way he wanted it to be, and reading *Harold and the Purple Crayon* confirmed for me something I already knew: like Harold, I was an artist.

I grew up in Pocomoke, Maryland, and started painting in watercolor and photo collage when I was about fifteen. I guess you could say it's just my way of looking at the world. When I start a book, I look through magazines for colors and patterns that might inspire me. I never know what I'm going to find. Once I used chocolate bars to make buildings. I like seeing things in new ways. If you turn a familiar image sideways or upside down, you can be surprised by what you see. If you tear up your art and glue it back together, the art changes. It becomes bigger and has more purpose.

I paint to jazz music, and all I hear is layers of sound. I see things in layers, and that's what is appealing to me. I see myself as putting together a world, and I just put all the things that I like in that world.

Peter Sís began his career as a filmmaker, and his film work is in the permanent collection at the Museum of Modern Art, New York.

This etching, entitled **Rhinoceros,** *by Albrecht Dürer, German painter and engraver (1471–1528), inspired Peter Sís to become an artist.*

Peter Sís

It was a long time ago, when I was little boy, that somehow, somewhere, I saw Albrecht Dürer's engraving of a rhinoceros from the Middle Ages. We lived in Czechoslovakia, which was under the control of the Communist party at that time. I probably saw the rhinoceros in a museum in Prague. I didn't see it in a book. We didn't have many books. This

picture was pure magic. Mysterious and beautiful. It was everything I found, and still find, inspiring about art. The rhinoceros became this exotic, fairy-tale mascot of mine. I drew the rhinoceros over and over. It became a symbol of me. This is hard to explain: In that society, where everyone was carefully guarding against showing any true feelings, the rhino became a perfect symbol of the tender soul and heart, protected from the outside world by its thick skin. The horn: Was it a vicious, threatening dagger or the magic horn of a unicorn? No wonder I used an image of the rhinoceros in ballet shoes, balancing on the rope above the abyss, as the first drawing I did when I left Prague and came to America.

I wanted to create a children's book about a rainbow rhinoceros. Like me, he was sort of lonely, curious, and well-meaning. When he was happy, his horn glowed with the colors of the rainbow. The story was quite long and complex; I thought it was the best story ever. I was young and daring, so I fully expected that my book would become a bestseller and make me rich and famous. I went to New York to show the story to almost all the children's book publishers, who in turn explained to me why they would not publish it. However, one of them agreed to work with me, and together we shaped the story into *Rainbow Rhino*, my first book. She has been my editor ever since.

Chris Raschka

The Happy Stone Age Children, or *Die fröhlichen Steinzeitkinder*, by Bertil Almqvist, is the first book I remember reading. My copy of the book, which I still have today, is written in German, though probably it was originally published in Swedish. Why did I have a German book on my bookshelves when I was young? Because the first place I went to school, and the first place I was given reading lessons, was in a town in Germany called Marburg. Folks there spoke German, though my family also spoke English, having come from Chicago. Of those first reading lessons, I have a memory of pretty, dark letters on creamy white pages opposite blue pictures. When my family moved back to Chicago, I brought some books with me, including this one. It's still one of my favorites.

I liked it then and I like it now because the story and drawings are simple and clear. They are also funny. The drawings carefully show what is going on, who is who, and what the places look like. That's all. And that's enough.

The story of *The Happy Stone Age Children* is pretty simple. In the Hedenho family, there are two children: big brother, Sten, and little sister, Flisa, and their parents, Knuta and Ben. The drawings show us their funny little Stone Age toys, their funny little house, which is a cave, of course, and their pets. Their beautiful dog is named Urax. The children even have a horse; they ride him using the horse's mane and tail as seat belts. Everything is lovely until the children ask for one pet too many: a wild boar. This eventually leads to the Hedenho family's flight from their happy island home to a new home across the sea, far from the boar: an island shaped like a sea serpent.

Bertil Almqvist's own drawings for *The Happy Stone Age Children* are so beautiful, I didn't want to change them. But I did want to change the shape of the book itself, so I made a little accordion book. In making my version, I studied the original drawings line by line. Then I painted these scenes into my handmade book. So now I have a handy accordion book, a condensed version of *The Happy Stone Age Children*, by Bertil Almqvist, that I can carry with me.

In re-imagining The Happy Stone Age Children, *Chris Raschka changed the shape of the original and created an accordion book.*

Chris Raschka's copy of The Happy Stone Age Children, *by Bertil Almqvist, which he still has today, is written in German, though probably it was originally published in Swedish.*

Yumi Heo grew up in Korea and carried her favorite book of folktales with her everywhere.

The collection of Korean folktales that Yumi Heo loved as a child didn't have any interior illustrations, a sharp contrast to the colorful books she creates today.

Yumi Heo

Throughout my childhood in Korea, I spent most of my time playing outside with my two younger brothers and friends. Ponds, streams, mountain hillsides, and the paths between rice paddies were our playground.

In the spring, after school, we would go to the pond near my house and watch tadpoles and tiny fish swimming around. I always brought my favorite book of Korean folktales with me. I would read it over and over. Back then we didn't have many picture books.

I especially liked stories about tigers, rabbits, turtles, and frogs. And I would imagine that I was the human character in the stories. Sometimes I would be the girl who climbed up the rope to the sky, trying to get away from the tiger, as in one of my favorite stories, "The Sun and the Moon."

Since then, I have always wanted to become an artist so that I could express my wondrous imagination visually on white paper.

SPECTACLES
FOR YOU

It must be the Land of Oz," said Dorothy "and we are surely getting near the Emerald City." They soon saw a beautiful green glow in the sky just before them. Yet it was afternoon before they came to the great wall that surrounded the City.

Robert Sabuda

When I was a boy, *The Wonderful Wizard of Oz*, by L. Frank Baum, was my favorite book. Growing up in the rural farm country of Michigan, I could completely empathize with Dorothy and her situation. It seemed like there was nothing to do and nothing exciting ever happened. I ached to be whisked away to a fantastic world where scarecrows talked, lions cried, and all it took was a bucket of water to finish off a wicked witch.

When I was eight years old, I began making pop-ups from old filing folders that my mother brought home from work. After teaching myself how to make simple pop-ups, I decided to create a book. I didn't even hesitate when coming up with a title: *The Wonderful Wizard of Oz!*

I spent weeks cutting and folding paper to re-create the world I loved so much in pop-up. Why I chose such a difficult story to retell I'll never know! Finally it was complete and, with its first perusal, the critic within me was born. The cyclone did not spin the way I wanted it to, so I completely abandoned pop-ups for the next twenty years!

But with the one-hundredth anniversary of *The Wonderful Wizard of Oz* approaching in the year 2000, I knew I wanted to be a part of the celebration. So I decided to create a *real* pop-up version of my all-time favorite book. And this time the cyclone *does* spin!

You can make your own pop-up Emerald City from *The Wonderful Wizard of Oz* like the one shown here {at near left}. Just visit www.RobertSabuda.com for a cutout pattern and step-by-step instructions. And always remember, "There's no place like home!"

Robert Sabuda began making books as a young child and first discovered pop-up books in the waiting room of his dentist's office.

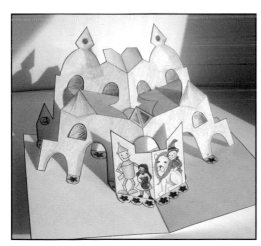

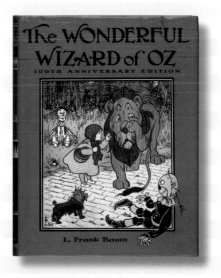

The Wonderful Wizard of Oz, *by L. Frank Baum, was published in 1900 and made into a motion picture in 1939. This facsimile of the original edition was published to commemorate the 100th anniversary.*

William Joyce remembers two great art teachers, Mrs. Hogan and Mrs. Slagle, who encouraged him to try all the mediums: watercolors, oils, pencils, pastels, charcoal, wood, canvas, and paper.

Maurice Sendak received the Caldecott Medal for his classic children's book, Where the Wild Things Are, *published in 1963.*

William Joyce

I first read Maurice Sendak's *Where the Wild Things Are* when I was a really little kid. I got lost in that book and haven't come out since.

My drawings in high school {see below, left} and college {below, center} were overwhelmingly influenced by Maurice's work and I knew it.

In time I found my own style, but there's still a little Max in everything I do. {See below, right, from my first book, *George Shrinks*.}

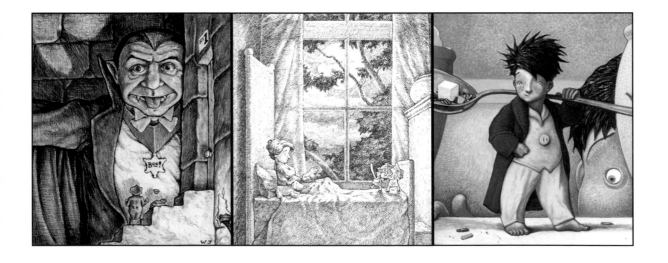

That very night in Max's room a forest grew

Paul O. Zelinsky painted into his flowers the faces of children who visited the Reading Is Fundamental event at the Corcoran Museum, Washington, D.C.

The Color Kittens, *by Margaret Wise Brown, illustrated by Alice and Martin Provensen, was published in 1949.*

The Color Kittens is a book written by Margaret Wise Brown and illustrated by Alice and Martin Provensen, but

Paul O. Zelinsky

in my four-year-old world it wasn't written or illustrated by anybody: It existed as a fact of nature. Obvious questions like "What are color kittens?" and "Why is it that they had to mix all the colors in the world?" never occurred to me. Primal, mythlike, the color kittens took their place among life's great mysteries. I thought they were dressed as train engineers. The book's plot has the kittens trying and trying to mix green. In a way, the book was written to teach facts about color, but its real subject is the huge pleasure to be found in the seeing and the feeling of color—the particularity and the deliciousness of fish-green and plum-purple and pig-pink. And if the kittens'—and my—delight in that deliciousness wasn't the only reason that I became a painter, it certainly was an early nudge in that direction.

Thinking about *The Color Kittens* and their paint cans, I remember one evening in art school when my studio mate filled an empty paint jar with acrylic medium and set a bunch of irises in it. He thought the flowers might draw the liquid plastic up into them, creating plastic flowers. The blue jar and the purple irises looked so beautiful that I started to paint the scene. I painted all night, faster and faster as the plastic-flower experiment failed and the flowers began to droop.

Today, musing on the rich experience of color and on paint cans and nurture and growth, I started to picture this scene in which the color kittens have arranged bunches of flowers in paint cans of different colors, and I just let the idea grow, to see what would happen with it.

The COLOR KITTENS

64 ■ *The Art of Reading*

A dedicated animal lover, Stephen Huneck frequently incorporates animals into his work. Favorite subjects include his dogs and cat.

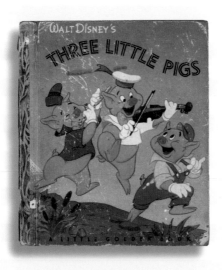

This edition of The Three Little Pigs *was adapted by Milt Banta and Al Dempster from the 1933 Walt Disney motion picture* The Three Little Pigs.

Stephen Huneck

When I was a boy, I would babysit for my four younger sisters and my baby brother by reading to them. My favorite book to read out loud was *The Three Little Pigs*. It is a great book to ham up with all the huffing and puffing and blowing your house down. I also loved the old-fashioned pictures in the book. The illustrations fascinated me and made me want to be an artist when I grew up so I could create my own pictures. Happily, that is exactly what I did. I became an artist. Now I make woodcut-print pictures to go with the stories I write.

To create a woodcut print, I first do a drawing of the future print in pencil, then I lay out all the different shapes, colors, and textures. The result is a series of carved blocks, one for each color in the print. After a block has been inked with its respective color, acid-free archival paper is laid onto the block and then hand-rubbed. I repeat the process for each color block. When this process is completed, I hang the prints to dry. That's how I made this print of me reading to my dog. Altogether I carved fourteen blocks of wood to create this print.

A few years ago, I discovered that my dogs greatly enjoyed my reading to them. My dogs love the attention and don't mind when I stumble over a word or two. They also like *The Three Little Pigs* with all the huffing and puffing and blowing the house down. My black Lab, Sally, is very smart. She gives me a little nudge when it's time to turn the page. Why don't you try reading to your dog? I bet you both will love it!

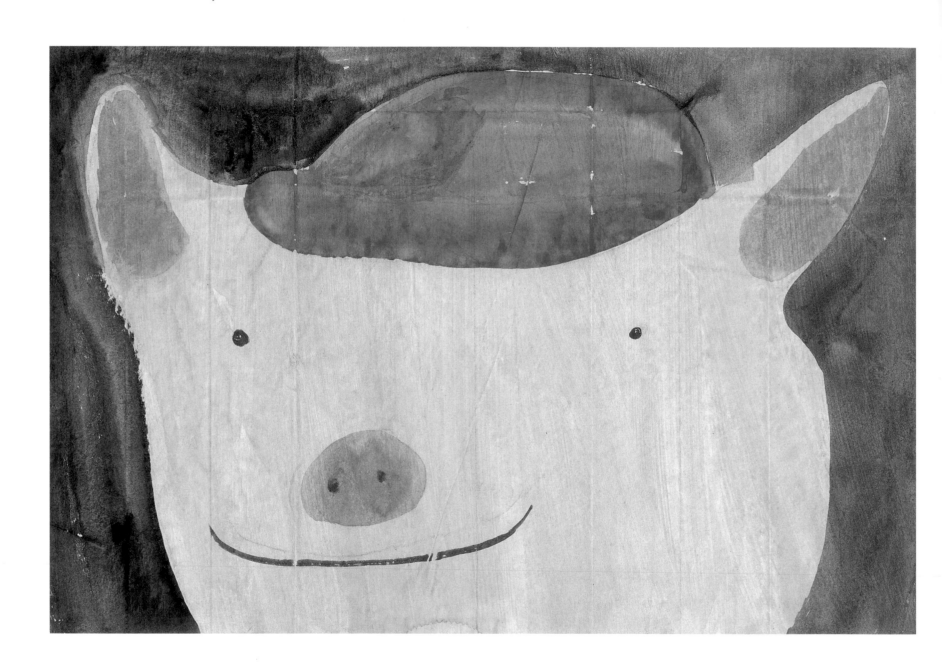

Douglas Florian

When I was growing up in the 1950s, there was one particular book I recall that seemed to inform, entertain, and fascinate me: *How Big Is Big? From Stars to Atoms*. Written by Herman and Nina Schneider and illustrated by Symeon Shimin, this nonfiction book explored size relationships and the concept of relativity for a young child. The straightforward text and black-and-white drawings progressed in scale from two children who have outgrown their clothes to the enormity of stars, touching upon elephants, trees, skyscrapers, and mountains along the way. The book then reversed direction and scaled down page by page to the unseen smallness of atoms. Facts were interspersed throughout, though some now seem dated: "It would take you four whole days and nights to fly around the earth."

Years later I created my own picture book of size-wise relativity: *A Pig Is Big*. Though not consciously based upon *How Big Is Big?*, my book also explores a progression of scale. With full-color illustrations and humorous verse, I move in size from pig to cow, and from cow to car, leading eventually to the entire universe. I don't reverse course toward the small, but close with a star constellation of a pig.

Though scientists today explore subatomic "charmed" particles and parallel universes in string theory, the simple charm of *How Big Is Big?* is still evident, as my ten-year-old son, Or, found out on his recent reading of the book.

Poet/artist Douglas Florian says there's only one rule he follows when writing poems: There are no rules. Poetry rules!

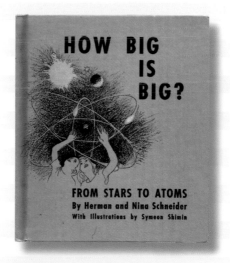

How Big Is Big? From Stars to Atoms, *by Herman and Nina Schneider and illustrated by Symeon Shimin, was first published in 1946 and is available through libraries and used-book stores.*

Loren Long is comforted by the thought that his grandma read **The Little Engine That Could** *to his mother when she was a little girl, just as his mother read it to him when he was young.*

The Little Engine That Could, *by Watty Piper, with illustrations by George and Doris Hauman, was published in 1930.*

Loren Long

She would start with a soft whisper . . . *I think I can, I think I can, I think I can* . . . slowly her voice would grow . . . *I think I can, I think I can, I think I can* . . . until finally with resolute confidence . . . *I think I can, I think I can, I think I can.*

Even today as an all-grown-up person, I can still hear my mother's voice and that familiar cadence as she would read those powerful words to me. I can see the rocking chair we would sit in together, and I still feel the warmth of those moments.

Though multitudes of people have read *The Little Engine That Could*, by Watty Piper, spanning many generations, when I was a young boy it seemed to have been written and created only for me. It was my book, it was my story, and it was my message.

I loved the spunk of Little Blue, and her willing determination has inspired and actually sustained me in some pretty harrying instances throughout my life. The story is about the power of a positive mental attitude. It is about trying to achieve something that seems impossible.

So as you go about the business of growing up, when something seems particularly challenging and difficult, remember Little Blue and whisper quietly to yourself . . . *I think I can, I think I can, I think I can* . . . and more times than not, you'll eventually hear yourself whispering back . . . *I thought I could, I thought I could, I thought I could.*

I'm comforted by the knowledge that my grandma read *The Little Engine That Could* over and over to my mother all the way back in the 1940s, when she was a little girl. My mother then read it to me time and time again when I was little. I have now read it to my little boys over and over again. And one day perhaps, my two sons will read *The Little Engine That Could* again and again to their own children . . . my grandkids.

Aren't books great!!!

Mark Teague

I have always loved books, but when I was a kid I lived in C. S. Lewis's Narnia. My favorite book in the series was *The Silver Chair*. I read it over and over again. At night, riding home through the southern California backcountry with my family, I was actually in the northern wastes of Narnia with Eustace and Jill and their guide, Puddleglum. When the travelers encounter the Lady of the Green Kirtle and her mysterious dark knight, the children are enchanted by the lady's musical laugh and charming words. Puddleglum, typically, remains skeptical. And rightly so. The Lady is an evil witch, and her advice leads them into grave danger.

For me, Puddleglum is the best character in children's books. Part man and part frog, tall and dour in appearance, his outrageous pessimism conceals a deep courage. He adheres to a simple philosophy: "I'm a chap who always likes to know the worst and then put the best face I can on it." As a kid I found his resolute gloominess oddly comforting. I still do.

When Mark Teague was young, he taught himself to draw. He wrote his own stories and drew pictures for them.

The Silver Chair, *by C. S. Lewis, with illustrations by Pauline Baynes, was published in 1953 and is the sixth book in* **The Chronicles of Narnia** *series.*

*Pat Cummings was born in Chicago.
Her family moved often because her
father was in the army. They lived
in Germany, in Japan, and in
several different states.*

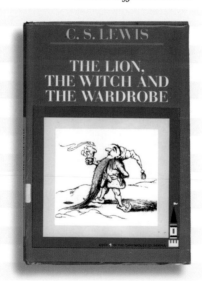

The Lion, the Witch and the
Wardrobe, *by C. S. Lewis, illustrated
by Pauline Baynes, is Book 1 in*
The Chronicles of Narnia *series.*

Pat Cummings

When Lucy first stepped through the closet into Narnia in *The Lion, the Witch and the Wardrobe*, all I wanted to do was go with her. I was about nine years old and living overseas in Okinawa, Japan, where everything seemed mysterious and magical. So *The Chronicles of Narnia* series, by C. S. Lewis, was right up my alley.

Lucy's first minute in Narnia, her meeting with Mr. Tumnus the Faun under the falling snow, created an image in my mind that has always stayed with me. As strange as it may have been for Lucy to find another world waiting right beyond her door, that moment under the lamppost seemed quietly cozy and inviting. The snow and the lamplight and the silent trees created such a hush that a friendly conversation with a passing Faun seemed perfectly natural.

I've always suspected there is magic right below every surface or beyond every door. The world would be seriously too serious without it.

And ever since I went through the back of the closet with Lucy, I've found that reading and writing, drawing and painting are surefire ways to sneak a peek at the other side. There is magic, and you can get there.

As a child, Kevin Hawkes loved to draw and paint. In art class he tried all kinds of projects, including sculpture with clay, plaster, wire, and papier-mâché.

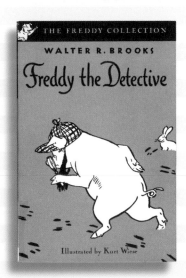

Freddy the Detective, *written by Walter R. Brooks, was published in 1932 and is the third in the Freddy series, which consists of twenty-six titles in all.*

Kevin Hawkes

I first met Freddy the Pig when I was in third grade. I was just becoming a serious reader. I had just finished all the Cowboy Sam books and was ready for something more challenging. I spotted Freddy on the school library shelf and took him home. Wow! The book was great! Freddy the Detective was funny and smart and brave (but not too brave). And all these animals were talking! Jinx the Cat and Charles the Rooster and Mrs. Wiggins the Cow.

I couldn't get enough of Freddy and rushed back to the library for more. Soon I was stopping by the library every afternoon and lurking around the Freddy section, waiting for some other kid to bring back the next exciting mystery for Freddy and me to solve. The librarian kept an eye out for any Freddy books and kept them for me at the desk.

Now that I think of it, *Freddy the Detective*, by Walter R. Brooks, was the first really "long" book that I had ever read. It opened my eyes to a strange and delightful place, a farm in upstate New York where animals talked and had adventures and solved mysteries. It was my first experience with fantasy fiction, yet Freddy seemed more real to me than any other character I had ever met. I began wondering what else in the world was more than it appeared to be, and so began a lifetime love of books. After that, I devoured books—everything I could get my hands on. That has made such a big difference in my life.

I especially love Kurt Wiese's illustrations for the Freddy books. He really made Freddy come to life for me. I re-imagined the cover of *Freddy the Detective* with Freddy casting a shadow of a young boy in a Sherlock Holmes costume. The boy is me, searching for clues as to where the next Freddy mystery might be!

Growing up, Mark Buehner received much encouragement from his teachers, who acknowledged him early on as a wonderful artist.

Gwendolyn the Miracle Hen, *by Nancy Sherman, illustrated by Edward Sorel, was published in 1961 and is now out of print. This copy was found through Browse About Book Exchange in North Wilkesboro, North Carolina, www.abebooks.com, just one of many rare- and used-book stores available online.*

Mark Buehner

When I was child, I had a handful of picture books that I loved. One in particular that stands out in my mind is *Gwendolyn the Miracle Hen,* written by Nancy Sherman and illustrated by Edward Sorel. To the best of my recollection, my mother responded to a magazine offer to join a book club that each month for one year would mail a children's picture book to your home. So every month a new book would arrive in the mail, wrapped in sturdy cardboard. *Gwendolyn the Miracle Hen* was one of the books I received. The story is about a poor farmer who doesn't have enough money to pay his rent, so his hen Gwendolyn comes to the rescue. She begins laying beautifully patterned eggs that the farmer is able to sell for one dollar each.

I remember poring over the illustrations and thinking that they were so beautiful, particularly the page that showed a close-up of some of those amazing eggs.

Years later, after I was married, my mother asked if I would like to take the books that held memories for me as a child. I found a few, but *Gwendolyn the Miracle Hen* was noticeably absent. After doing some searching around Mom's house, I figured that perhaps Mom had given it away to one of my nieces or nephews, and that the book was gone. A number of times over the years I mentioned the book to my wife and told her how much I had enjoyed it as a child. Last year for Christmas, she surprised me with a copy of the book that she had been able to track down on the Internet. Now I'm enjoying those amazing eggs all over again. What great fun!

Dick Bruna

My family owned a publishing business, so I was familiar with books and authors from a very early age. I cherished books and would go to the library often. I was drawn to and always looked at the pictures before reading the story. I loved poetry and adventures, especially journeys that included animals. Some of my favorite books were the *Babar* tales by Jean de Brunhoff. (He is also one of my favorite artists.)

The first editions of the *Babar* books were oversized, and the pictures appeared—at least to me—larger than life. The spacious composition allowed me to feel like I was part of the story. I felt like I was in the jungle with Babar, making friends along our journey. Most of the time, I created my own stories to go with the pictures. I felt a bit afraid but secure in the knowledge that I was safe at home. It was magical! I will never forget the sense of security and the endearing cast of characters from these books.

When I create illustrations for my books, I strive to impart the same experience: a world in which children feel safe yet which provides them with enough space to use their imagination. The adventures happen close to home; the surprising is found in the everyday. The secret of their success lies in their simplicity—strong black lines and clear, lively colors. Visual language is very important, and children have a good grasp of it.

Dick Bruna cherished books as a child and would often visit the library. He would always look at the pictures first before reading the story.

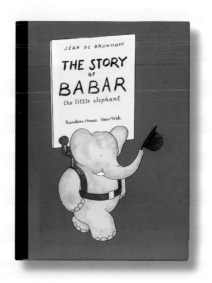

The Story of Babar *was created by pianist Cecile de Brunhoff to entertain her two sons at bedtime. The next day, the children told the story to their father, artist Jean de Brunhoff, who wrote it down and illustrated it.*

Tony DiTerlizzi recalls how his mother would read to him and his sister every night before bed.

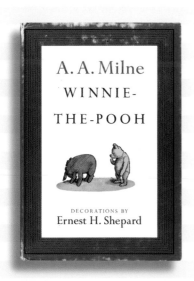

Winnie-the-Pooh was written by A. A. Milne and first published in England in 1926.

In Which
Tony DiTerlizzi Reflects on Some Old Friends As He Tries to Create Some New Ones

Tony DiTerlizzi

It was nine o'clock at night. My bedroom was lit by a single lamp sitting on my battered white dresser. Under the sheets and blankets of my little bed, my sister was cuddled up next to me. She was fidgety and could not seem to get comfortable. I was ready to draw the imaginary-line border with my finger, indicating "my area" that could not be crossed by anyone, let alone her.

But before I could, our mom walked in and flopped down on the bed next to us. She didn't get under the covers; instead she sat upright, resting against the headboard. We put our heads in her lap and got as close as we possibly could, excited with anticipation.

She opened an old, dog-eared book and asked which story we would like to hear: "In Which Eeyore Loses a Tail and Pooh Finds One" or "In Which Piglet Meets a Heffalump"? Instantly we were there, in A. A. Milne's Hundred Acre Wood, frolicking with Christopher Robin and all his friends. It was a magical time when I could hear his words through my mother's voice as I drifted off to sleep.

I would revisit the enchanted woods many times, even though I "outgrew" the stories. (Can you imagine carrying a copy of *Winnie-the-Pooh* around in high school? It was bad enough I was an art geek with oversize glasses.) But the cast of characters seemed so familiar. I knew grumpy people like Eeyore, excitable characters like Tigger, and many times I felt as meek and little as Piglet. Though all these personalities got along in the end, Milne had woven them together in a fashion very similar to life—they each had foibles, they conspired against one another, they faced disaster, but somehow they continued on.

I know what you are thinking: All this heart and soul in a bunch of stuffed animals and woodland creatures? Yes, and it was all brought to vivid life with Ernest H. Shepard's delightful little scribbly drawings (which look very simple, but take a lifetime to render as masterfully as he did). The humor of Milne's text somehow seeped into Shepard's drawings, as the two acted as one in bringing these stories to life. It was true magic to my six-year-old eyes, and still is thirty years later. It was something I wanted to be: a Teller of Tales, a Transporter of Young Imaginations, an A. A. Milne and an E. H. Shepard.

As a child, David Kirk loved to draw, and he spent hours drawing robots. He was also good at making things by hand.

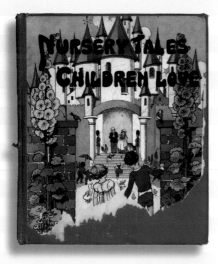

Thumbelina *was written by Hans Christian Andersen in 1835 and is one of the author's most popular fairy tales.*

David Kirk

Hans Christian Andersen's fairy tale *Thumbelina* was one of my favorite stories from childhood. I loved stories about fairies and angels, stories of sacrifice and redemption. Fantasy and legends fascinated me. My parents were professional puppeteers, so our house was filled with stories.

I'm not sure when I began to love bugs. I know that by kindergarten I was catching big praying mantises in the local ditch, but I assume I was interested before that. I think all kids realize what special creatures bugs are. They're like tiny aliens on Earth, so different from us—not unlike little Thumbelina, who was born in a flower. That's why I decided to show them together here; to me, they're from the same place, the place where fantasy and reality blend.

In addition to fairy tales and fantasy, I loved robots as a child. I had always thought that I became interested at age five, when my brother got a toy robot for Christmas. Recently, though, I found that some of my earliest drawings—ones I did when I was three or four years old—were of robots. When I was six, I got my own first robot. After that, I spent all my time drawing robots or searching them out in dime stores. To this day, I still have dreams of finding robot toys under cabinets in obscure dime stores, and of coming across Thumbelina reading to her friends, the caterpillars, in the woods.

Susan Jeffers

Some of my favorite childhood memories are of my mother and father reading to my sister and me at bedtime. Sometimes, while my mom read, my dad embellished the stories with tap dances and walking on his hands. This was in the days before television, when we depended on our own ingenuity for entertainment and creative satisfaction. Our parents read to us from our storybook collection, *My Book House.* The books were illustrated with beautiful, small ink drawings. These black-and-white illustrations sometimes had a spot of color—maybe blue or orange—that was it.

Looking back now, I realize I did not miss the bigger color pictures we now have in books. Those small, spare illustrations left my imagination free to create. This ability came into good use when, as a teen, I struggled to stay awake through the Reverend Stoneton's sermons. High in the choir loft, I would tell myself stories, creating in my imagination all the pictures that were not included in *My Book House.*

Our mother was an artist, and the house was always full of projects: decorating-the-front-door contest for the Garden Club, costumes for the town thespians, and yearly fire-prevention poster contests. She shared her delight in her vision and in our visions, and her passion for a job well done. With all our experience at home, my sister and I were designated class artists throughout our school years. It was easy for me, therefore, to decide as a sophomore in high school that I wanted to go to art school at Pratt Institute. When I got my first job in publishing, I realized picture books were the perfect combination of my favorite things: literature, including the stories of my childhood, and art.

I have drawn my favorite picture from *Thumbelina.* This particular scene illustrates Thumbelina being saved by the swallow from a dismal existence—married to a mole and living underground. *Thumbelina* fascinated me. I wanted to be as brave as she was and as loyal as she was to her friend, the swallow.

What I am always looking for in a story is whether it moves me, changes my view of the world, or simply makes me laugh. I believe, at their best, art and literature encourage our inner growth, offer a resting place for us, and help us become whole. Reading is the key.

Susan Jeffers and her sister were designated class artists throughout their school years.

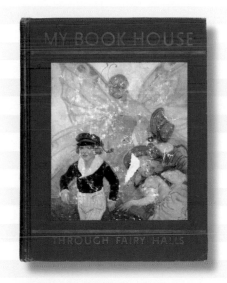

Thumbelina, *by Hans Christian Andersen, is one of the many stories collected in* Through Fairy Halls, *volume six of* My Book House. *Edited by Olive Beaupré Miller, the multi-volume set was in print from 1920 through 1971.*

Ivan Velez, Jr.

When I was about eight years old, my mother gave me a huge dictionary of mythological creatures she had inherited from a neighbor lady, and I was hooked. Half-human beasts, flying or crawling demigods, women who bore monsters that ate heroes—all erasing the dull, angry world around me and replacing it with . . . well, with wonder and hunger for more. After that, the hunt began. Thank God for candy stores with comic books—and for little local libraries.

Our library was very brown, and nothing special. It was too cold in the winter and too warm in the summer. It was never particularly well kept, and the people who worked there seemed tired and overburdened—it was the Bronx in the late sixties, and everyone looked that way—but they were good with the books, and that was what really mattered.

I found the story of the Little Mermaid in a well-worn collection of mermaid stories. I resisted the book at first; mermaid stories seemed too girlie, and the pages and pages of unadorned type scared me. But the librarian insisted, and she pushed until I relented. I wonder to this day if the library lady knew what she was doing when she handed me the book. Was that a sad little smile on her face when I took it from her hands?

Among the hunting mermaids who lured men to their death, vain mermaids who were destroyed by their own pride, magic mermaids who granted wishes in exchange for their lives, and hideous mermaids who destroyed all they touched, there was the most poignant mermaid of them all. The Little Mermaid's story hit me like a punch in the gut.

She was a creature of the sea that lacked a soul, and wanted one more than anything. In order to gain one, she would have to become human . . . but to become human, she would have to suffer without a sound . . . and if she didn't gain her man's undying love, she would die without a soul or a family.

Why would she barter so much away? She tried so hard, and lost it all, and even though she was rewarded for her suffering, in the end she still hadn't gotten what she wanted. And yet, her story remained beautiful and poetic. It was this story that made me look for the sad beauty in everything else I read—and try to create the same in what I wrote and drew.

Ivan Velez, Jr., was raised in the South Bronx and was heavily influenced by chopsocky karate flicks, **Astro Boy** *cartoons, Spanish soaps, and his local library.*

The Little Mermaid *was written in 1836. After reading the story, Ivan went on to devour more of Hans Christian Andersen's classic fairy tales.*

Gerald McDermott recalls many nights spent lying on the living-room floor, reading, while his parents sat nearby, reading their own favorite books.

The Childcraft books, first published in the 1920s and reprinted many times, featured nursery rhymes and poetry, folk and fairy tales, myths and legends.

Gerald McDermott

There were many evenings during my childhood when my father, my mother, and I would gather together in the small living room of our home in Detroit, Michigan. There was no television set, the radio was turned off, and the house was quiet. My father would be sitting in his easy chair, reading his book; my mother sat on the sofa, reading her book; and I was stretched out on the floor, reading my book. Each of us was immersed in his or her own reading while bound together in silent communion. That was the still center from which my thoughts went spiraling upward and outward, around the world and through the universe, circling back to our little house to fire my creative imagination.

In a modest household, our treasures were our books. These included a popular series of classics, a small collection of contemporary novels, and special books for me. At one time, my father even had the notion of selling Childcraft books in his spare time to supplement his income. The Childcraft books, first published in the 1920s and reprinted many times in the following decades, featured nursery rhymes and poetry, folk and fairy tales, legends and myths. The hardbound volumes had covers colored a deep, bittersweet orange and were profusely illustrated. In the end, my dad sold just one set: to us.

Of the many illustrations in the Childcraft books, the image that accompanied the myth of Jason and the Argonauts has remained vividly in my memory. It showed Jason's ship, the *Argo*, plying the seas and approaching the shores of Colchis. There, a sleeping dragon, coiled around a tree, guarded the object of Jason's quest—the Golden Fleece. Though perhaps magnified and altered by memory (I haven't seen that book in fifty years), this is the image from my childhood love of reading that I've chosen to illustrate. The loneliness of the voyage, the danger of the quest, the excitement of recovering the treasure: these were the elements that were irresistible to me in childhood and became metaphorical of my journey as an artist.

Dan Yaccarino

When I was young, all I wanted to do was draw pictures and make up stories. Needless to say, I spent most of my free time hard at work at my drawing table with all of my art supplies around me.

Every week without fail, my mother would take my brother, my sister, and me to the library. There are two things that I remember about those Saturday mornings: first, I would check out the absolute most books allowed; and second, in that massive stack of books, there would always be at least one by author-illustrator Robert Tallon. I doubt anyone else ever got to read any of his books, since they were always in my possession.

I read every one of his books that the library had. I read *Latouse My Moose, Rhoda's Restaurant,* and *Zoophabets,* but my favorite was *The Thing in Dolores' Piano.* I couldn't get enough of that darn book! I must have read it a million times. It was by far the weirdest story I had ever read, which was probably why I loved it so much.

Dolores was a little girl who was a rotten pianist, and no one could stand to listen to her lousy playing. Not only did her playing offend those around her—the notes inside the piano couldn't stand it, either! I had never read a book whose main character was not likable or friendly. Dolores was so obnoxious that her only friend was her dog—and that was only because he was tone-deaf. The one thing she had going for her was that she was brave. Dolores wanted to play her piano so badly that when the notes refused to play, she ventured inside the piano.

How was I supposed to know that you could do something as fun as writing and illustrating children's books for a living? What a relief it was to find out that I didn't have to be an insurance-claims adjuster or a dentist when I grew up. Whew!

It was through this book, and others by many other authors and illustrators, that I drew inspiration and confidence. They showed me that I could indeed follow my dream of creating stories and pictures for kids just like me.

And now all I want to do is draw pictures and make up stories. Needless to say, I spend most of my free time hard at work at my drawing table with all of my art supplies around me.

Dan Yaccarino now lives down the street from Robert Tallon, author of his favorite childhood books.

Now out of print, **The Thing in Dolores' Piano,** *by Robert Tallon, was published in 1970.*

About the Illustrators

MARY AZARIAN has illustrated over forty books, including the Caldecott Medal–winning title *Snowflake Bentley*, by Jacqueline Briggs Martin, and *Miss Bridie Chose a Shovel*, by Leslie Connor.

DIANA CAIN BLUTHENTHAL is the author and/or illustrator of several children's books, including *A Tiger Called Thomas*, by Charlotte Zolotow; *Meaner Than Meanest*, by Kevin Somers; and her own books, *I'm Not Invited?*; *Matilda the Moocher*; *The Youngest Fairy Godmother Ever*; and *Hot Fudge Hero*.

DICK BRUNA has written and illustrated almost one hundred books for young children. Some of his famous creations include Snuffie the Dog, Poppie Pig, the bears Boris and Barbara, and his most renowned character, Miffy, the white bunny. *Miffy and Friends* also appears on the educational-television network Noggin.

ASHLEY BRYAN's *Beat the Story-Drum, Pum-Pum* won the Coretta Scott King Award, while *Lion and the Ostrich Chicks and Other African Folk Tales*, *Ashley Bryan's ABC of African American Poetry*, and *What a Morning! The Christmas Story in Black Spirituals* were all selected Coretta Scott King Honor Books. In 1990, Mr. Bryan received the Arbuthnot Prize, one of the highest honors in children's literature.

MARK BUEHNER and his wife, Caralyn, have created several picture books, including *Superdog: The Heart of a Hero* and *Snowmen at Night*. Mr. Buehner has also illustrated popular books by various authors, including *The Adventures of Taxi Dog*, by Debra and Sal Barracca; *Harvey Potter's Balloon Farm*, by Jerdine Nolan; and *Niccolini's Song*, by Chuck Wilcoxen.

LYNNE CHERRY is the author and/or illustrator of over thirty award-winning books for children, including *A River Ran Wild; The Armadillo from Amarillo;* and *The Great Kapok Tree*. Author of her own environmental newsletter for children, she is also the founder of the Orion Center for Children's Environmental Literature.

HENRY COLE's books include such beloved titles as *Four Famished Foxes and Fosdyke; Livingston Mouse; Some Smug Slug; The Worrywarts;* and *Barefoot: Escape on the Underground Railroad*, all written by Pamela Duncan Edwards. He is the author and illustrator of his very own *I Took a Walk* and *Jack's Garden*.

BRYAN COLLIER is the illustrator of a number of award-winning books, including *Uptown*, which he also wrote; *Freedom River* and *Martin's Big Words: The Life of Dr. Martin Luther King, Jr.*, both by Doreen Rappaport; and *Visiting Langston*, by Willie Perdomo. Mr. Collier was awarded a Caldecott Honor for *Martin's Big Words* and has received the Coretta Scott King Award and Honor several times.

RAÚL COLÓN has received a Gold Medal and a Silver Medal from the Society of Illustrators. His books include *My Mama Had a Dancing Heart*, by Libba Moore Gray, a *New York Times* Best Illustrated Book; *Always My Dad*, by Sharon Dennis Wyeth; and *A Weave of Words: An Armenian Tale*, by Robert D. San Souci.

PAT CUMMINGS illustrated the Coretta Scott King Award winners *My Mama Needs Me*, by Mildred Pitts Walter, and *Storm in the Night*, by Mary Stolz. She is also the author-illustrator of *My Aunt Came Back* and *Angel Baby* and serves as an instructor of children's book illustration at the Parsons School of Design.

DAVID DIAZ has been an illustrator and graphic designer for more than twenty years. In addition to receiving the 1995 Caldecott Medal for *Smoky Night*, by Eve Bunting, Mr. Diaz has garnered honors from *Parents' Choice, American Illustration, Communication Arts,* the American Institute of Graphic Arts, and the New York Art Directors Club.

TONY DiTERLIZZI created artwork for games such as *Dungeons & Dragons, Planescape,* and *Magic: The Gathering* before writing and illustrating children's books. His illustration of Mary Howitt's classic poem *The Spider and the Fly* won him a Caldecott Honor. He recently teamed up with friend Holly Black to create the well-loved *Spiderwick Chronicles*.

RICHARD EGIELSKI was awarded the Caldecott Medal for his illustrations in *Hey, Al,* written with Arthur Yorinks. Mr. Egielski's books include *The Tub People* and *The Tub Grandfather*, both by Pam Conrad. *Buz* and *Jazper*, which he wrote and illustrated, were named *New York Times* Best Illustrated Books for Children.

LOIS EHLERT is the author and illustrator of many acclaimed books for young chil dren, including *Color Zoo,* a Caldecott Honor Book. Some of her other bestselling books include *Eating the Alphabet; Snowballs; Fish Eyes;* and *Waiting for Wings.* Her work has appeared in countless publications and has received numerous awards and honors.

DOUGLAS FLORIAN is the author-illustrator of many books of poetry for middle-grade and younger readers, including *Mammalabilia; Insectlopedia; Winter Eyes;* and *Vegetable Garden.* Mr. Florian won the Lee Bennett Hopkins Poetry Award and received an ALA Notable Children's Book Award for *Beast Feast.*

KEVIN HAWKES is the illustrator of over thirty acclaimed picture books and chapter books, including *The Librarian Who Measured the Earth,* by Kathryn Lasky, and *Sidewalk Circus,* by Paul Fleischman. Mr. Hawkes won the prestigious Kate Greenaway Medal for his illustration of *Weslandia,* also by Paul Fleischman.

YUMI HEO was born and raised in Korea, where she studied graphic design. Books she has written and illustrated include *Father's Rubber Shoes* and *The Green Frogs: A Korean Folk Tale.* She is the illustrator of many books, including *The Lonely Lioness and the Ostrich Chicks: A Masai Tale,* by Verna Aardema, and *So Say the Little Monkeys,* by Nancy Van Laan.

STEPHEN HUNECK's award-winning children's books include *My Dog's Brain; Sally Goes to the Beach; Sally Goes to the Mountains;* and *The Dog Chapel.* His work is exhibited in museums around the world, including the Smithsonian Institution in Washington, D.C., and the Museum of American Folk Art in New York City.

SUSAN JEFFERS's list of distinguished picture books includes *Cinderella; Thumbelina; My Pony;* the *McDuff* series, by Rosemary Wells; and *Stopping by Woods on a Snowy Evening,* by Robert Frost. Her awards include a Caldecott Honor for *Three Jovial Huntsmen* and the ABBY Award for *Brother Eagle, Sister Sky.*

WILLIAM JOYCE is the author and illustrator of such acclaimed books as *Dinosaur Bob; Santa Calls;* and *The Leaf Men and the Brave Good Bugs.* His illustrations have also graced many covers of *The New Yorker.* Two of his books, *George Shrinks* and *Rolie Polie Olie,* have been adapted as animated television series, and his book *Buddy* was made into a live-action film. He also created pre-production art for the animated film *Toy Story.*

STEVEN KELLOGG's own stories and much-loved retellings such as *Johnny Appleseed; Paul Bunyan; Pecos Bill; Chicken Little;* and *A Hunting We Will Go!* He is also the illustrator of *A Beasty Story,* by Bill Martin Jr.; *The Rattlebang Picnic,* by Margaret Mahy; and *Is Your Mama a Llama?,* by Deborah Guarino.

DAVID KIRK, the celebrated creator of the bestselling *Miss Spider* picture books, began making toys and art for children over fifteen years ago. He also designs furniture, one-of-a-kind toys, and paintings treasured by collectors.

NINA LADEN's books include *Roberto: The Insect Architect,* which won a Silver Medal from the Society of Illustrators; *Bad Dog,* an *American Bookseller* Children's Pick; *When Pigasso Met Mootisse,* an *American Bookseller* Pick of the Lists; and *The Night I Followed the Dog,* which received a 1994 *Parents' Choice* Award.

LOREN LONG has worked as a freelance illustrator since 1992 and in that time has been honored with two Gold Medals from the Society of Illustrators in New York. His books include *When I Heard the Learn'd Astronomer,* by Walt Whitman; *Mr. Peabody's Apples,* by Madonna; and *I Dream of Trains,* by Angela Johnson.

FRED MARCELLINO was considered the preeminent American book-jacket artist and designer of the 1970s and 1980s before he turned his talents to the art of making picture books. He was awarded a Caldecott Honor for his first picture book, *Puss in Boots,* by Charles Perrault. His other books include *The Wainscott Weasel* and *A Rat's Tale,* both by Tor Seidler; *The Story of Little Babaji; Ouch!,* by Natalie Babbitt; and *I, Crocodile,* which he also wrote. A revolutionary force in the fields of book design and children's book illustration, Fred Marcellino died in 2001.

GERALD McDERMOTT's numerous picture books include *Creation.* His work has garnered many honors, among them the Caldecott Medal for *Arrow to the Sun: A Pueblo Indian Tale* and Caldecott Honors for *Raven: A Trickster Tale from the Pacific Northwest* and *Anansi the Spider: A Tale from the Ashanti.* A Joseph Campbell Foundation fellow, Mr. McDermott lives in California. (www.geraldmcdermott.com)

DAVID McPHAIL is an illustrator well known for his adorable animal characters, including his series of books about Emma the Bear and Pig Pig. He has written and illustrated over fifty award-winning books for children, including *Mole Music; Edward and the Pirates; Henry Bear's Christmas; Pigs Aplenty, Pigs Galore!; Pig Pig Rides; Pig Pig Grows Up;* and *Fix-it.*

PAUL MEISEL is the illustrator of many beloved children's picture books, including *Go to Sleep, Groundhog!,* by Judy Cox; *We All Sing with the Same Voice,* by J. Phillip Miller; *Go Away, Dog,* by Joan Nodset; *How to Talk to Your Cat,* by Jean Craighead George; *Coco and Cavendish,* by Judy Sierra; and *Lunch Money: Poems About School,* by Carol Diggory Shields.

JERRY PINKNEY is the recipient of four Caldecott Honors for *Noah's Ark; John Henry,* by Julius Lester; *The Talking Eggs,* by Robert D. San Souci; and *Mirandy and Brother Wind,* by Patricia C. McKissack. His work has also been recognized with a Coretta Scott King Award three times and a Coretta Scott King Honor twice.

PATRICIA POLACCO grew up with storytellers and began writing and illustrating books for children when she was forty-one years old. She has created many picture books, including *Chicken Sunday; Thunder Cake; Rechenka's Eggs;* and *The Keeping Quilt.*

CHRIS RASCHKA, writer, illustrator, and trained violist, was awarded a Caldecott Honor for *Yo! Yes?* in 1993. *Mysterious Thelonious,* one of a series of books on jazz greats, and *A Poke in the I* have been named *New York Times* Best Illustrated Books.

Painter and printer **ERIC ROHMANN** is the author and illustrator of the 2003 Caldecott Medal winner, *My Friend Rabbit.* Mr. Rohmann made his children's-book illustration debut with the innovative *Time Flies,* a wordless picture book awarded a Caldecott Honor in 1999. He is also the creator of the critically acclaimed *The Cinder-Eyed Cats.*

Often referred to as the "Prince of Pop-ups," **ROBERT SABUDA** is the best-known pop-up book artist working today. He is the creator of the remarkable *America the Beautiful; Alice's Adventures in Wonderland; The Wonderful Wizard of Oz;* and *The Night Before Christmas.*

BRIAN SELZNICK's first book, *The Houdini Box,* won the Texas Bluebonnet Award and the Rhode Island Children's Book Award. Among his most recent books are *The Meanest Doll in the World,* by Ann M. Martin and Laura Godwin; *Amelia and Eleanor Go for a Ride* and *When Marian Sang,* both by Pam Munoz Ryan; and *Walt Whitman: Words for America* and *The Dinosaurs of Waterhouse Hawkins,* a Caldecott Honor book, both by Barbara Kerley.

PETER SÍS has more than twenty books to his credit, including *Starry Messenger: Galileo Galilei,* a Caldecott Honor title; *The Tree of Life: Charles Darwin;* and *The Train of States.* He has won the *New York Times* Best Illustrated Book of the Year five times and was awarded a MacArthur Fellowship in 2003.

MARK TEAGUE is the illustrator of such popular and award-winning books as *How Do Dinosaurs Say Good Night?; Dear Mrs. LaRue: Letters from Obedience School;* the *Poppleton* series; and the *First Graders from Mars* series.

IVAN VELEZ, JR. is the creator of *Tales of the Closet,* a graphic series about the lives of gay teens in New York City. Mr. Velez has worked for DC and Marvel Comics. He has written several Milestone titles, especially *Blood Syndicate,* and had a year-long run writing *Static Shock* comics. His work has appeared in *Gay Comics, Details* magazine, and on HBO.

DAVID WIESNER has been awarded two Caldecott Medals: one for *The Three Pigs* and the other for *Tuesday.* He also received a Caldecott Honor twice, for *Sector 7* and again for *Free Fall.* An exhibit of his original artwork, *Seeing the Story,* toured the United States in 2000 and 2001.

ASHLEY WOLFF is the illustrator of many award-winning children's books, including the popular *Miss Bindergarten* series, by Joseph Slate. Ms. Wolff also illustrates her own acclaimed stories, among them *Me Baby, You Baby; Stella and Roy;* and *Stella and Roy Go Camping.*

DAN YACCARINO is an artist, writer, producer, and creator of his own animated television series. He has written and illustrated over thirty children's books, including *Good Night, Mr. Night; Unlovable; Trashy Town;* and *Zoom! Zoom! Zoom! I'm Off to the Moon!*

PAUL O. ZELINSKY was awarded the Caldecott Medal for his book *Rapunzel* and is the illustrator of three Caldecott Honor titles: *Rumpelstiltskin; Hansel and Gretel,* retold by Rika Lesser; and *Swamp Angel,* by Anne Isaacs. He is the adapter and illustrator of many popular books and stories, including *The Wheels on the Bus.*

Index

■ By Title